# THE WIZARD'S BACK

## by Brant Parker and Johnny Hart

FAWCETT GOLD MEDAL • NEW YORK

*THE WIZARD'S BACK*

ISBN: 0-449-13654-X

19   18   17   16   15   14   13

First Fawcett Gold Medal printing: August 1973

Printed in the United States of America

4-25

5-30

5-31

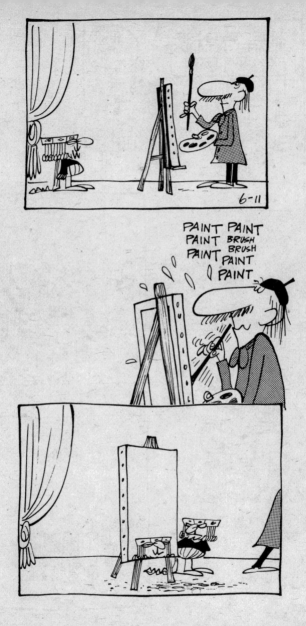

8-15

11-4

11·25

# MORE MAGIC
# FROM THE
# WIZARD OF ID

EVERY MAN IS INNOCENT UNTIL
PROVEN BROKE   13650   $1.50

I'M OFF TO SEE THE WIZARD   13700   $1.50

THE KING IS A FINK   13709   $1.25

LONG LIVE THE KING   13655   $1.50

THE PEASANTS ARE REVOLTING   13671   $1.50

REMEMBER THE GOLDEN RULE   13717   $1.50

THERE'S A FLY IN MY SWILL   13687   $1.50

THE WIZARD OF ID #8   13681   $1.25

THE WIZARD OF ID—YIELD   13653   $1.50

THE WIZARD'S BACK   13654   $1.50

THE WONDROUS WIZARD OF ID   13648   $1.50

This offer expires 1 September 81                    8065